You Are an Ironman: A Comprehensive Training Guide for
First-Time Ironman Finishers

By: Taylor Reed
Edited & Published by: Creative Pages

You Are an Ironman by Creative Pages Publisher

You Are an Ironman by Creative Pages Publisher

Welcome to Creative Pages!

Discover a World of Creativity and Inspiration

At Creative Pages, we're passionate about crafting journals and books that cater to a variety of needs and interests. Whether you're seeking a thoughtful journal to capture your ideas, a low-content planner to organize your days, or an immersive read to dive into, we have something for everyone.

What We Do:

- **Journals:** Designed to inspire and motivate, helping you capture your thoughts, dreams, and daily reflections.
- **Low-Content Books:** Perfect for those who need guided prompts, planners, and trackers to stay organized and productive.
- **Mid-Content Books:** Engaging content with a balance of structure and creativity for a richer experience.
- **High-Content Books:** Immersive reads that offer a deep and engaging experience.

Don't Miss Out!

Browse Our Full Range on Amazon & Try Our Other Books and Journals:
Discover new favorites and essential tools for your daily life and creative journey.

Join Our Community!

- **Follow Us on Instagram:** Stay updated on new releases, special offers, and behind-the-scenes content. Follow us at @creativepagespublisher and become part of our vibrant community!
- **Get in touch:** We'd love to hear from you! For any questions, feedback, or collaborations, email us at creativepagespublisher@gmail.com

You Are an Ironman by Creative Pages Publisher

You Are an Ironman by Creative Pages Publisher

OUTLINE

Chapter 1: Introduction to Ironman	7
Chapter 2: Training Plans for First-Time Ironman Athletes	15
Chapter 3: Nutrition Strategies for Ironman Success	25
Chapter 4: Mental Preparation and Mindset for Ironman Competitors	35
Chapter 5: Gear Essentials: What to Buy for Your First Ironman	45
Chapter 6: Overcoming Common Challenges in Ironman Training	55
Chapter 7: Ironman Race Day Logistics and Tips	65
Chapter 8: Triathlon Swimming Techniques for Beginners	75
Chapter 9: Cycling Tips for New Ironman Participants	85
Chapter 10: Running Strategies to Complete Your First Ironman	95
Chapter 11: Conclusion and Final Thoughts	105
Training Plans for Beginners	113

You Are an Ironman by Creative Pages Publisher

Chapter 1: Introduction to Ironman

What is an Ironman?

An Ironman is one of the most formidable endurance challenges in the world of triathlons, designed for athletes who seek to test their limits. This grueling race consists of three segments: a 2.4-mile swim, a 112-mile bike ride, and a 26.2-mile marathon run, completed in that order. The total distance of 140.6 miles must be tackled within a specified time limit, usually 17 hours. For first-time athletes, understanding the structure and demands of an Ironman is crucial for effective training and successful completion. Each leg of the race not only requires physical stamina but also strategic planning in terms of pacing, nutrition, and mental resilience.

Training for an Ironman necessitates a well-structured plan that encompasses various elements, including swimming, cycling, and running workouts. First-time athletes often benefit from gradually increasing their distances and intensity, leading up to race day. This progressive training approach not only builds endurance but also allows the body to adapt to the rigors of the race. Incorporating brick workouts—training sessions that combine two disciplines, such as cycling followed by running—can be particularly beneficial in preparing the body for the unique transitions between the race segments.

Nutrition plays a pivotal role in Ironman preparation and performance. As you train for such an extensive event, understanding what, when, and how to eat can significantly impact your energy levels and recovery. First-time participants should focus on developing a nutrition strategy that includes balanced meals, hydration plans, and race-day fueling techniques. Practicing these strategies during training sessions is essential, as it allows athletes to identify what works best for them and to avoid gastrointestinal distress on race day.

Mental preparation and the right mindset are often overlooked aspects of Ironman training. The race is as much a mental challenge as it is a physical one. First-time athletes should cultivate mental resilience through visualization techniques, positive affirmations, and setting realistic goals. Developing coping strategies for moments of fatigue or discomfort during training can also prepare athletes for the inevitable challenges they will face during the race. Embracing the mental aspect of Ironman training can help foster a more confident and focused approach to the event.

Finally, becoming familiar with race day logistics and gear essentials is critical for first-time Ironman athletes. The right equipment, from wetsuits to bikes and running shoes, can enhance performance and comfort. Additionally, understanding the race course, transition areas, and aid stations can alleviate anxiety and allow athletes to concentrate on their performance. By addressing these logistical details and ensuring that all gear is in top condition, first-time participants can significantly enhance their overall Ironman experience, making the journey to the finish line more enjoyable and fulfilling.

The Ironman Experience

The Ironman experience is a unique and transformative journey that extends far beyond the race itself. For first-time athletes, preparing for an Ironman triathlon encompasses a blend of physical training, nutritional strategies, mental fortitude, and logistical planning. Each segment of the race—swimming, cycling, and running—demands a specific set of skills and preparation. This subchapter will explore what you can expect throughout this demanding yet rewarding process, emphasizing how thorough preparation can enhance your experience and performance on race day.

Training for an Ironman is often described as a rigorous yet exhilarating endeavor. First-time athletes will find themselves engaging in a structured training plan that gradually builds endurance and strength over several months. This plan will typically include a mix of long-distance workouts, speed sessions, and recovery days, aimed at enhancing your performance across all three disciplines. It's essential to listen to your body during training, allowing for rest and recovery, which are crucial for preventing injury and ensuring that you're race-ready. The training experience is not only about physical preparation; it also serves as a mental rehearsal for the challenges you will face on race day.

Nutrition plays a pivotal role in both training and race day success. As you ramp up your training volume, your dietary needs will change significantly. First-time Ironman athletes must focus on fueling their bodies with the right balance of macronutrients—carbohydrates, proteins, and fats. Understanding how to properly hydrate and replenish electrolytes during training and the race is equally important. Experimenting with various nutrition strategies during training will help identify what works best for you. This preparation allows you to fine-tune your race day nutrition plan to avoid gastrointestinal issues and sustain energy levels throughout the event.

Mental preparation cannot be overlooked in the Ironman experience. Completing such a grueling race requires not only physical strength but also a resilient mindset. Visualization techniques, positive self-talk, and goal-setting strategies can enhance your mental toughness. Athletes often encounter psychological barriers during training and on race day, such as fatigue, self-doubt, or the temptation to quit. Developing coping mechanisms and mental strategies will help you push through these challenges. Engaging in mindfulness practices can also aid in maintaining focus during long training sessions and the race itself, allowing you to stay present in the moment and manage stress effectively.

On race day, the logistics of the Ironman experience come into play, and being well-prepared can greatly reduce anxiety. From setting up your transition area to understanding the race course and timing, familiarity with the race day process is crucial. Athletes should arrive early to acclimate themselves to the environment, review the course maps, and participate in the pre-race briefings. Having a checklist for gear essentials ensures that you won't forget critical items, such as your wetsuit, bike, and running shoes. Finally, remember that the Ironman experience is a celebration of your hard work and dedication. Embrace the journey, focus on your goals, and savor the accomplishment of crossing the finish line, knowing you have prepared thoroughly for this life-changing event.

Why Choose an Ironman?

Just to hear the famous sentence when you cross the finish line "[Your Name], YOU ARE AN IRONMAN." Just kidding. Or actually not, as this has been selected on many surveys as the main motivator for many athletes.

Anyway, choosing to participate in an Ironman triathlon is a significant decision that can transform not only your physical fitness but also your mental resilience and overall lifestyle. For first-time athletes, the allure of conquering such a challenging event often stems from the desire to push personal boundaries, achieve fitness goals, and experience the exhilaration of crossing the finish line. The Ironman distance—2.4-mile swim, 112-mile bike ride, and a 26.2-mile run—represents a test of endurance and determination that can instigate profound personal growth.

One of the most compelling reasons to choose an Ironman is the sense of community that comes with it. As you embark on your training journey, you'll likely find yourself surrounded by fellow athletes who share similar goals and challenges. This camaraderie can provide invaluable support and motivation, making the arduous training process more enjoyable. Whether it's through local training groups, online forums, or race-day meetups, the relationships formed during this journey can last a lifetime, fostering friendships built on shared experiences and mutual encouragement.

In addition to community support, participating in an Ironman offers a structured approach to fitness that can lead to significant health benefits. The rigorous training required helps improve cardiovascular health, build muscular strength, and enhance overall stamina. As you follow a comprehensive training plan, you will not only develop your physical capabilities but also learn about nutrition strategies essential for sustaining energy throughout the event. Understanding how to fuel your body effectively can lead to long-term dietary improvements, making you a more conscious and healthy eater even beyond race day.

Mental preparation is another crucial aspect of training for an Ironman. The physical demands are substantial, but the mental challenges can be just as formidable. First-time athletes often discover that developing a strong mindset is key to overcoming obstacles and setbacks. Techniques such as visualization, goal setting, and positive self-talk can significantly impact your performance, helping you stay focused and resilient, even when the training gets tough. Embracing these mental strategies not only prepares you for race day but also equips you with tools to handle challenges in everyday life.

Lastly, participating in an Ironman provides an opportunity for personal achievement like no other. Completing an event of this magnitude is a testament to your hard work, dedication, and perseverance. The sense of accomplishment that comes with crossing the finish line can boost self-confidence and inspire you to tackle future challenges, both in athletics and in life. By choosing to compete in an Ironman, you are not just signing up for a race; you are

You Are an Ironman by Creative Pages Publisher

committing to a journey that will enrich your life in numerous ways, encouraging growth, resilience, and a profound sense of fulfillment.

Chapter 2: Training Plans for First-Time Ironman Athletes

Understanding the Ironman Race Format

The Ironman race format is a challenging yet rewarding test of endurance that consists of three distinct disciplines: swimming, cycling, and running. Specifically, an Ironman event features a 2.4-mile swim, a 112-mile bike ride, and a 26.2-mile marathon run, all completed in succession. Understanding this format is crucial for first-time athletes, as it not only helps in planning a training regimen but also sets the stage for effective race day strategies. Each segment of the race demands unique physical and mental preparation, making it essential to familiarize yourself with the intricacies of the Ironman format.

Starting with the swim, it is important to recognize that this first leg often sets the tone for the rest of the race. Athletes typically begin in waves, which helps manage the number of participants in the water at any one time. The swim can be intimidating due to the distance and the chaotic nature of race starts. First-time athletes should focus on developing efficient swimming techniques, such as proper breathing, stroke form, and sighting to stay on course. Incorporating open-water swim practice into your training will also help you acclimate to the conditions you will face on race day.

Transitioning from the swim to the bike is a critical aspect of Ironman racing. This segment is known as T1, and it requires athletes to efficiently change gear and prepare for the cycling portion. Proper planning for this transition can save valuable time. It is advisable to practice transitions during training to become familiar with the process and to identify any gear essentials you may need. During the bike leg, pacing is paramount; athletes must find a balance that conserves energy for the marathon that follows. Nutrition strategies, such as consuming electrolytes and carbohydrates, should also be integrated into your cycling training to ensure you are fueled and hydrated.

As athletes complete the cycling leg, they will transition to running in T2. This is another critical point in the race, where fatigue can start to set in. Mental preparation plays a vital role here, as the shift from cycling to running can be challenging. Athletes should expect their legs to feel heavy and may need to adjust their mindset to tackle the marathon portion. Employing mental strategies, such as breaking the run into smaller segments or using positive self-talk, can help maintain motivation and focus throughout this final leg of the race.

Finally, understanding the overall race logistics and how to navigate the course is essential for first-time Ironman athletes. Familiarizing yourself with the race venue, water stops, and aid stations can greatly enhance your experience and performance. Knowing where to expect support, as well as when to hydrate and refuel, will contribute to your success. Additionally, reviewing race day tips, such as arriving early and thoroughly checking your gear, can alleviate stress and boost your confidence. With the right preparation and understanding of the Ironman race format, you'll be well on your way to crossing the finish line and celebrating your accomplishment.

Building Your Training Schedule

Creating a training schedule for your first Ironman is a critical step that sets the foundation for your success on race day. As a first-time athlete, it's essential to understand that an effective training plan balances swim, bike, and run workouts while incorporating adequate rest and recovery. A well-structured schedule will not only prepare your body for the demands of the Ironman but also help you manage your time effectively, ensuring that you can juggle training with work and personal commitments.

Start by determining how many weeks you have before race day. Most first-time Ironman athletes benefit from a training cycle of 20 to 30 weeks. This extended period allows you to build endurance gradually while minimizing the risk of injury. Break down your training into phases: base building, intensity, and tapering. The base phase focuses on building your aerobic capacity and endurance, while the intensity phase incorporates speed work and race-specific training. Finally, the tapering phase reduces training volume to help your body recover and prepare for optimal performance on race day.

When designing your weekly training plan, allocate specific days for each discipline: swimming, cycling, and running. A common approach is to dedicate three days to each sport, with a long workout for each discipline on the weekends. For instance, Saturday could be your long bike ride, while Sunday might be reserved for a longer run. Incorporate transition practice between disciplines to simulate race conditions, as this will enhance your efficiency on race day. Additionally, consider including strength training and flexibility sessions to support your overall fitness, focusing on core strength and injury prevention.

Nutrition plays a vital role in your training schedule. As you ramp up your training volume, your nutritional needs will change. It's essential to fuel your body adequately before, during, and after workouts. Plan your meals and snacks around your training sessions to ensure you have the energy required for each workout. Experiment with different foods and hydration strategies during your long workouts to identify what works best for you. This preparation will help you avoid gastrointestinal issues on race day and ensure you can maintain your energy levels throughout the event.

Lastly, prioritize recovery in your training schedule. Rest days are just as important as your training sessions, allowing your body to heal and adapt to the increased workload. Listen to your body and adjust your training intensity as needed. If you're feeling fatigued or experiencing pain, don't hesitate to take an extra rest day or modify your training plan. Building a training schedule is not solely about intensity and volume; it's about creating a sustainable plan that allows you to progress steadily while enjoying the journey toward becoming an Ironman athlete.

Balancing Swim, Bike, and Run Training

Balancing swim, bike, and run training is a crucial aspect of preparing for your first Ironman. As a first-time athlete, understanding how to allocate your training time effectively across these three disciplines can significantly influence your performance on race day. Each sport demands different physical and mental capacities, and finding the right mix will not only enhance your endurance but also help prevent burnout and injury. This subchapter will guide you through the principles of balancing your training regimen, ensuring you approach each discipline with the attention it deserves.

To create a balanced training plan, begin by assessing your current fitness levels in each discipline. If you are stronger in one area—perhaps you have a background in cycling or swimming—you might want to allocate slightly more training time to running, which is often the most challenging segment for new athletes. Aim for a weekly structure that includes dedicated swim, bike, and run sessions, while also incorporating rest and recovery days. A common approach is the "three-week build, one-week recovery" model, where you gradually increase your training load over three weeks followed by a lighter recovery week. This strategy not only helps to build endurance but also allows your body to adapt and recover.

In addition to time allocation, consider the specifics of your training sessions. Quality often trumps quantity; therefore, it's essential to focus on the effectiveness of each workout. For swimming, incorporate drills that enhance your technique and efficiency, as mastering proper form can significantly improve your speed and reduce energy expenditure. For cycling, mix long rides with interval training to build both endurance and power. Running sessions should vary as well, including long runs, tempo runs, and brick workouts, where you transition directly from cycling to running to simulate race day conditions. This variety keeps your training engaging while addressing the different demands of each discipline.

Nutrition plays a pivotal role in supporting your training regimen. As you balance swim, bike, and run sessions, ensure your diet is rich in carbohydrates, proteins, and healthy fats to fuel your workouts and facilitate recovery. Pay attention to hydration strategies, especially during longer sessions, as dehydration can impair performance and recovery. Consider experimenting with different types of fuel—gels, bars, and electrolyte drinks—during your training to determine what works best for your body before race day. Proper nutrition will not only enhance your physical performance but also support your mental resilience as you tackle the demands of Ironman training.

Finally, remember that mental preparation is key to achieving balance in your training. It's common for first-time athletes to feel overwhelmed by the volume and intensity of Ironman training. Developing a positive mindset and establishing realistic goals will help you stay focused and motivated. Practice visualization techniques, where you mentally rehearse your swim, bike, and run segments, creating a mental blueprint for success. By maintaining a balanced approach to your training—combining effective workouts, proper nutrition, and mental fortitude—you will set yourself up for a rewarding and successful Ironman experience.

Periodization and Recovery

Periodization is a crucial aspect of training for first-time Ironman athletes. It involves structuring your training into distinct phases that focus on specific goals, allowing for systematic progression and recovery. Typically, periodization is divided into three main phases: the preparation phase, the build phase, and the peak/race phase. Each of these phases serves a unique purpose in developing your endurance, strength, and race-specific skills. For beginners, understanding the concept of periodization can help prevent burnout and injuries, ultimately leading to a successful race day experience.

In the preparation phase, the focus is on building a solid aerobic base. This is where endurance training takes precedence, involving longer, low-intensity workouts that enhance your cardiovascular fitness. During this phase, it is essential to incorporate a balanced approach to nutrition, ensuring that your body receives the necessary fuel to recover and adapt to the increasing demands of training. A well-rounded diet rich in carbohydrates, proteins, and healthy fats will support your energy levels and facilitate recovery. Consider consulting a sports nutritionist to tailor your dietary needs to your training schedule.

The build phase ramps up the intensity and volume of your training. During this period, you will begin to incorporate more race-specific workouts, such as interval training, tempo runs, and brick workouts that combine cycling and running.

Recovery remains a key focus, as the increased workload can lead to fatigue and potential overtraining. To optimize recovery, include rest days in your training plan and prioritize sleep. Recovery techniques, such as foam rolling, stretching, and even massage, can help alleviate muscle soreness and improve flexibility, allowing you to bounce back stronger for your next workout.

As you approach the peak/race phase, your training should become more focused and specific to the demands of the Ironman. This phase is characterized by tapering, where you gradually reduce your training volume to allow your body to recover and prepare for race day. This is a critical time to fine-tune your nutrition strategies, ensuring your body is primed for the performance ahead. Hydration and carbohydrate loading in the days leading up to the race are essential components that can significantly impact your race performance. Additionally, mental preparation becomes increasingly important during this phase as you visualize your race strategy and build confidence in your abilities.

Recovery does not end once you cross the finish line; it is an ongoing process. Post-race recovery is just as vital as the training itself. After completing an Ironman, your body will need time to heal and rebuild. Focus on hydration, nutrition, and gentle movement to aid in recovery. Listening to your body and allowing adequate time for rest will help prevent injuries in future training cycles. Embracing periodization and prioritizing recovery throughout your journey will not only enhance your performance but also foster a sustainable training practice that encourages long-term success in the sport of triathlon.

At the end of this book, in the chapter callled Training Plans, you will find some of the best free training plans for first-time Ironman athletes. Feel free to use them and modify them as needed using the advice given on Chapter 2.

Chapter 3: Nutrition Strategies for Ironman Success

Fundamentals of Endurance Nutrition

Endurance nutrition is a vital component of your preparation for an Ironman, as it directly impacts your performance and recovery during training and on race day. Understanding the fundamentals of what to eat, when to eat, and how to fuel your body can make the difference between finishing strong and struggling to cross the finish line. For first-time Ironman athletes, a well-structured nutrition plan not only supports your training efforts but also enhances your overall experience in the race.

The foundation of endurance nutrition lies in macronutrients: carbohydrates, proteins, and fats. Carbohydrates are crucial for endurance athletes, as they serve as the primary source of energy during prolonged physical activity. It is essential to prioritize complex carbohydrates, such as whole grains, fruits, and vegetables, in your daily diet. These foods provide sustained energy release, which is particularly important during long training sessions. Proteins play a significant role in muscle repair and recovery, while healthy fats contribute to overall energy levels and endurance. Balancing these macronutrients ensures that your body is well-equipped to handle the demands of your training regimen.

In addition to understanding macronutrient composition, timing your nutrition is equally important. Consuming the right foods at the right times can optimize your performance and recovery. For long training sessions, athletes should focus on pre-workout meals that are rich in carbohydrates and low in fat and fiber to avoid gastrointestinal discomfort. During training, incorporating easily digestible snacks or energy gels can help maintain energy levels. Post-workout, prioritize protein and carbohydrate intake to facilitate muscle recovery. Developing a nutrition schedule that aligns with your training plan will help you establish a routine that you can rely on come race day.

Hydration is another critical element of endurance nutrition. During an Ironman, athletes can lose significant amounts of fluid through sweat, making it essential to maintain proper hydration levels. Aim to drink water throughout your training sessions and incorporate electrolyte-rich drinks during longer workouts to replenish lost minerals. Understanding your hydration needs and monitoring your fluid intake can prevent dehydration, which can severely impact your performance and recovery. Experiment with different hydration strategies during training to find what works best for your body.

Finally, individualization is key when it comes to endurance nutrition. Every athlete has unique needs based on body composition, metabolism, and personal preferences. It is important to experiment with various foods and hydration strategies during training to determine what works best for you. Keeping a food journal can help you track your nutrition and its effects on your performance, allowing you to make adjustments as needed. By focusing on the fundamentals of endurance nutrition and tailoring your approach, you will be better prepared to tackle the challenges of your first Ironman, ensuring that both your body and mind are ready to perform at their best.

Pre-Race Nutrition Plan

The Pre-Race Nutrition Plan is a critical component of your preparation as a first-time Ironman athlete. Proper nutrition in the days leading up to the race can significantly impact your performance and overall experience. This plan is designed to help you understand the importance of fueling your body correctly, ensuring that you arrive at the starting line feeling strong and ready to tackle the challenges ahead. By focusing on the right balance of carbohydrates, proteins, and fats, you can maximize your energy stores and maintain optimal hydration levels.

In the days leading up to race day, carbohydrate intake becomes essential. Carbohydrates serve as the primary energy source for endurance athletes, and increasing your carb consumption can help stockpile glycogen stores in your muscles and liver. Aim to shift your diet towards higher-carb options, such as whole grains, fruits, and vegetables, while still incorporating lean proteins and healthy fats. This strategy, known as carbohydrate loading, should begin about three days before the race, allowing your body to adapt and optimize energy availability for the event.

Equally important is hydration, which plays a pivotal role in your performance and recovery. Dehydration can severely hinder your ability to perform, leading to fatigue and decreased endurance. In the week leading up to the race, be vigilant about your fluid intake. Water is essential, but electrolyte-rich beverages can help maintain your sodium and potassium levels, which are vital for muscle function and preventing cramps. Monitor your hydration status by checking the color of your urine; light yellow indicates adequate hydration, while dark yellow suggests a need for more fluids.

On the eve of the race, it's crucial to focus on your pre-race meal. This meal should be consumed approximately three to four hours before the start and should consist of easily digestible, high-carb foods with moderate protein and low-fat content. Options like oatmeal, bagels with honey, or a banana with peanut butter can provide the necessary energy without causing gastrointestinal discomfort. Avoid high-fiber foods and heavy meals that could lead to bloating or cramping during the race. Remember, this is not the time to experiment with new foods; stick to familiar options that you know your body can handle.

Lastly, mental preparation is as important as physical readiness when it comes to nutrition. Visualize your pre-race routine, including your meals and hydration strategy. This mental rehearsal can help reduce anxiety and reinforce the importance of sticking to your nutrition plan. By understanding and implementing a solid pre-race nutrition strategy, you not only equip your body for the demands of the Ironman but also set yourself up for a positive race day experience. A well-executed nutrition plan can empower you to focus on your performance, allowing you to enjoy the journey and cross that finish line with confidence.

Nutrition During Training

Nutrition plays a crucial role in the training and performance of first-time Ironman athletes. As you embark on this demanding journey, understanding how to fuel your body effectively is essential for optimizing your training sessions, enhancing recovery, and ensuring peak performance on race day. The right nutrition strategies can help you build endurance, maintain energy levels, and reduce the risk of injury, making it imperative to pay attention to what you eat during this transformative period.

During training, your body undergoes significant physiological changes as it adapts to the rigors of endurance exercise. This adaptation process requires a well-balanced diet rich in macronutrients: carbohydrates, proteins, and fats. Carbohydrates serve as the primary energy source, particularly during high-intensity workouts. Aim to consume complex carbohydrates such as whole grains, fruits, and vegetables to provide sustained energy. Incorporating protein is also vital, as it aids in muscle recovery and repair. Sources such as lean meats, dairy, legumes, and plant-based alternatives should be included in your meals to support muscle growth and recovery. Healthy fats, found in nuts, seeds, avocados, and fish, are also an essential part of your diet, helping to provide long-lasting energy during long training sessions.

Hydration is another critical component of nutrition during training. As you train for extended periods, your body loses fluids and electrolytes through sweat. It's essential to develop a hydration plan that includes water and electrolyte-rich beverages to replace lost fluids. Pay attention to your body's thirst signals, but also proactively hydrate before, during, and after workouts. During longer training sessions, consider consuming sports drinks or electrolyte tablets to maintain optimal hydration levels and replenish essential minerals.

Timing your nutrition around your workouts can significantly impact your training effectiveness. Prior to training, consuming a meal or snack that includes carbohydrates and some protein will provide the necessary fuel for your session. Post-workout nutrition is equally crucial; aim to consume a balanced meal or snack that includes both carbohydrates and protein within 30 to 60 minutes after training. This timing helps replenish glycogen stores and kickstarts the recovery process, allowing your body to adapt and prepare for the next training session. Experiment with different foods and timing strategies to discover what works best for you and your unique needs.

Beyond physical nutrition, mental preparation also plays a vital role in your training journey. As you navigate the challenges of Ironman training, maintaining a positive mindset is essential. Nutrition can influence not only your physical performance but also your mental resilience. A well-nourished body supports cognitive function, mood, and motivation—key elements for overcoming obstacles and staying committed to your training plan. By prioritizing nutrition, you will not only enhance your physical capabilities but also cultivate the mental toughness necessary to tackle the demands of an Ironman event.

Race Day Nutrition Strategies

Race day nutrition is a critical component of your Ironman performance, especially for first-time athletes who may be navigating the complexities of fueling their bodies for such an extensive endurance event. Proper nutrition on race day not only supports physical performance but also helps to maintain mental focus and resilience throughout the long hours of swimming, cycling, and running. Understanding what to eat, when to eat, and how to hydrate can significantly impact your overall race experience and success.

As you prepare for race day, it's essential to develop a nutrition plan that aligns with your training. This involves practicing your nutrition strategy during long training sessions to identify what works best for your body. On race day, you should aim to consume a combination of carbohydrates, electrolytes, and fluids to sustain your energy levels. Carbohydrates are crucial, as they provide the quick energy your body needs to perform at its best. Aim for 60 to 90 grams of carbohydrates per hour, which can be achieved through a mix of energy gels, chews, and sports drinks that you have tested during training.

Hydration is another key element of race day nutrition. Dehydration can lead to decreased performance and fatigue, so it's vital to drink fluids regularly throughout the race. Pay attention to the weather conditions on race day, as heat and humidity can influence your hydration needs. A good rule of thumb is to drink about 500 to 750 milliliters (17 to 25 ounces) of fluid per hour, adjusting based on your sweat rate and environmental factors. Electrolyte balance is also crucial, as the loss of sodium and other electrolytes through sweat can lead to cramping and fatigue. Utilizing electrolyte tablets or sports drinks can help maintain this balance.

Pre-race nutrition is equally important. The meal you consume the night before and breakfast on race day can set the tone for your energy levels. A carbohydrate-rich dinner, such as pasta with a lean protein source, can provide the necessary fuel for the upcoming exertion. On race morning, aim for a light breakfast that is familiar to you, ideally consumed about two to three hours before the race starts. Foods such as oatmeal, bananas, or energy bars can provide the right balance of carbohydrates and prevent gastrointestinal distress during the event.

Finally, remember that flexibility in your nutrition strategy is vital. No two athletes are the same, and what works for one person may not work for another. Be prepared to adjust your intake based on how you feel throughout the race. Practice listening to your body during training to recognize signs of hunger, thirst, or fatigue. Developing a nutrition strategy that is personalized and adaptable will not only enhance your race day performance but also contribute to a more enjoyable experience as you cross the finish line of your first Ironman.

Chapter 4: Mental Preparation and Mindset for Ironman Competitors

The Importance of Mental Toughness

Mental toughness is a crucial component for first-time Ironman athletes, as it plays a significant role in both training and race day performance. This psychological resilience enables athletes to push through physical and emotional barriers, ensuring they stay focused on their goals despite the inevitable challenges that arise during preparation and competition. Developing mental toughness is not just about enduring pain; it's about cultivating a mindset that embraces adversity, harnesses motivation, and maintains a positive outlook throughout the demanding journey of training for an Ironman.

One key aspect of mental toughness is the ability to maintain focus under pressure. Training for an Ironman often involves long hours of swimming, cycling, and running, alongside managing life's other commitments. Athletes will encounter fatigue, discomfort, and moments of self-doubt. Developing strategies to sharpen focus, such as setting specific goals for each training session or visualizing success, allows athletes to navigate these challenges effectively. This mental discipline can make the difference between feeling overwhelmed and remaining determined to push through.

Another important element of mental toughness is resilience. The road to Ironman completion is often filled with setbacks, whether it's an injury, a poor performance in a training session, or unexpected life events. Resilience is the ability to bounce back from these obstacles, learn from them, and adapt. Athletes can cultivate resilience by maintaining a growth mindset—viewing challenges as opportunities for growth rather than insurmountable barriers. This shift in perspective fosters a more constructive approach to training and racing, helping athletes to remain steadfast in their pursuit of an Ironman finish.

Additionally, mental toughness is closely related to emotional regulation. The emotional rollercoaster of training can lead to frustration, anxiety, and even burnout if not managed properly. First-time Ironman athletes should develop techniques to regulate their emotions, such as mindfulness practices, breathing exercises, or journaling about their experiences. These strategies can help athletes recognize and process their feelings, allowing them to maintain a calm and focused mindset when faced with the pressures of training and competition.

Finally, the importance of mental toughness cannot be overstated on race day. The Ironman is not just a physical challenge; it is a test of mental fortitude. Athletes will face moments of fatigue, discomfort, and doubt during the event. Those who have cultivated mental toughness are better equipped to navigate these challenges, employing positive self-talk, visualization techniques, and pre-race routines to stay centered. By prioritizing mental preparation alongside physical training, first-time Ironman athletes can enhance their overall performance and experience, ultimately crossing the finish line with a sense of accomplishment and pride.

Visualization Techniques

Visualization techniques are powerful tools that can enhance your performance and mental readiness as you prepare for your first Ironman. These techniques involve creating vivid mental images of your training sessions, race day, and even the finish line, helping to reinforce your goals and boost your confidence. For first-time athletes, incorporating visualization into your training regimen can help to alleviate anxiety, improve focus, and create a positive mindset as you embark on this challenging journey.

To begin with, it's essential to understand the different types of visualization techniques available. One effective method is outcome visualization, where you picture yourself successfully completing the Ironman. Imagine crossing the finish line, feeling the joy and relief of achieving a monumental goal. This type of visualization helps to solidify your commitment to the training process and can inspire you to push through tough workouts. Another technique is process visualization, where you mentally rehearse specific aspects of your training and race day, such as swimming efficiently, maintaining a steady pace on the bike, or executing a strong run. This detailed mental practice can enhance your muscle memory and improve your performance on race day.

Incorporating these visualization techniques into your training schedule can be done in various ways. Set aside a few minutes each day to close your eyes and imagine yourself in different scenarios related to your Ironman journey. You might visualize your transition from the swim to the bike, feeling the exhilaration of the water and the power of your legs as you pedal. Alternatively, picture yourself tackling the run, focusing on your breathing and stride. The more detailed and vivid your mental images, the more effective the visualization will be. Make it a habit to engage in this practice regularly, especially before key workouts or long training sessions.

Additionally, visualization can be particularly beneficial when it comes to managing race day nerves. As you approach the event, anxiety can creep in, making it difficult to focus. By visualizing yourself calmly preparing for the race, setting up your gear in transition, and navigating the course, you can reduce pre-race jitters and create a sense of familiarity with the environment. This mental rehearsal can help you feel more in control and confident when it comes time to compete, allowing you to perform at your best when it matters most.

Finally, remember that visualization is not a replacement for physical training but rather a complementary tool that enhances your overall preparation. By integrating these techniques into your training plan, you will not only improve your mental resilience but also cultivate a deeper connection to your goals. Visualization allows you to mentally prepare for the physical and emotional challenges of the Ironman, ultimately setting you up for success on race day and beyond. Embrace these strategies as part of your journey, and watch as they transform your approach to training and competition.

Setting Goals and Managing Expectations

Setting goals and managing expectations is a crucial aspect for first-time Ironman athletes. As you embark on this challenging journey, it's essential to recognize that the road to an Ironman finish line is not just about physical endurance; it's also a mental and emotional journey.

Establishing clear, achievable goals will provide you with direction and motivation, while managing your expectations will help you navigate the inevitable ups and downs of training and racing.

When setting goals, it's important to differentiate between long-term and short-term objectives. Long-term goals might include completing your first Ironman within a specific time frame or qualifying for a subsequent race. These goals should be ambitious yet realistic, pushing you to achieve more while still being attainable. Short-term goals, on the other hand, can focus on daily or weekly training sessions, such as improving your swimming technique or completing a specific distance on your bike. By breaking down the larger goal into smaller, manageable objectives, you'll cultivate a sense of accomplishment that fuels your motivation and keeps you engaged in your training.

Managing expectations is equally important. As a first-time athlete, you may have visions of crossing the finish line with ease, but the reality is that training for an Ironman is a significant commitment that can test your physical and mental limits. Understand that setbacks, such as injuries or unforeseen life events, can occur. By acknowledging these challenges upfront, you can prepare yourself to adapt your training plan as needed. It's essential to maintain a flexible mindset, allowing yourself the grace to adjust your expectations based on your progress and circumstances.

Nutrition plays a vital role in your training and race day performance, which should also be factored into your goal-setting process. Aim to develop a nutrition strategy that supports your training regimen and aligns with your specific needs as an athlete. Setting goals related to your nutritional habits, such as experimenting with different fueling options during longer training sessions, can enhance your performance and bolster your confidence. Remember, what works for one athlete may not work for another, so be open to trial and error as you discover what best fuels your body.

Finally, mental preparation is an often-overlooked aspect of goal setting and expectation management. Visualization exercises can help you mentally rehearse your race day experience, preparing you for various scenarios you may encounter. This mental training can significantly impact your performance, especially when faced with challenges during the race. By cultivating a positive mindset and focusing on your progress rather than perfection, you'll find that you can approach your Ironman journey with resilience and enthusiasm, ultimately leading to a more rewarding and fulfilling experience.

Strategies to Overcome Mental Barriers

Mental barriers can be one of the most significant challenges for first-time Ironman athletes. As you embark on this demanding journey, it's crucial to recognize that mental fortitude is just as important as physical preparation. Understanding how to identify and overcome these barriers is vital to achieving success in your training and ultimately crossing the finish line. This subchapter will explore effective strategies to help you strengthen your mental resilience and maintain focus throughout your Ironman journey.

One of the most effective strategies for overcoming mental barriers is visualization. This technique involves imagining yourself successfully completing your training sessions and the race itself. Athletes can benefit from visualizing not only the finish line but also the process, including the swim, bike, and run segments. By creating a mental picture of success, you can boost your confidence and reduce anxiety. Regularly practicing visualization can help condition your mind to remain calm and focused, even during challenging moments in training or competition.

Another powerful strategy is the practice of mindfulness and meditation. These techniques can help you develop a greater awareness of your thoughts and feelings, allowing you to manage stress and anxiety more effectively. Incorporating mindfulness into your training routine—whether through breathing exercises, yoga, or meditation—can enhance your ability to stay present and focused. This focus can be especially beneficial during the grueling hours of training or the race itself, helping you push through discomfort and maintain your mental edge.

Establishing a strong support system can also play a crucial role in overcoming mental barriers. Surround yourself with fellow athletes, coaches, and friends who understand the demands of Ironman training. Sharing your experiences, fears, and triumphs with others can provide encouragement and motivation, reminding you that you are not alone in this journey. Participating in group training sessions or joining a local triathlon club can foster camaraderie and help you build relationships that will keep you accountable and uplifted throughout your preparation.

Lastly, setting realistic goals and celebrating small achievements along the way can significantly enhance your mental resilience. Break down your training into manageable milestones, such as completing a certain distance in swimming, cycling, or running. Acknowledging these successes, no matter how small, can provide a sense of accomplishment and boost your confidence. This approach not only alleviates the pressure of the overwhelming task ahead but also reinforces a positive mindset that will carry you through the challenges of Ironman training and race day. By implementing these strategies, you can effectively overcome mental barriers and prepare yourself for the exhilarating journey that lies ahead.

You Are an Ironman by Creative Pages Publisher

Chapter 5: Gear Essentials: What to Buy for Your First Ironman

Essential Swim Gear

Swim gear is an essential component of your preparation for an Ironman, as it not only enhances your training experience but also contributes significantly to your performance on race day. As a first-time Ironman athlete, investing in the right swim gear can make a considerable difference in your comfort, efficiency, and confidence in the water. This subchapter will guide you through the essential swim gear you should consider, helping you make informed decisions that align with your training goals.

A quality swimsuit is the foundation of your swim gear. Opt for a triathlon-specific wetsuit, which provides buoyancy and thermal insulation that can be invaluable during open water swims. A wetsuit designed for triathlons allows for maximum flexibility in the shoulders, facilitating a more natural swimming motion. Pay attention to the fit; it should be snug but not restrictive, allowing you to maintain a good range of motion. If you're training in warmer waters or during summer months, a speed suit or swim skin can be a great alternative, as it is designed to reduce drag while keeping you comfortable.

In addition to a wetsuit, investing in a good pair of goggles is crucial. Look for goggles that fit well and create a watertight seal to prevent leaks. Consider options with interchangeable lenses to adapt to varying light conditions, which can be particularly useful when training in different environments. Anti-fog and UV protection features are also important, ensuring that you can see clearly and are protected from the sun during your outdoor swims. Lastly, don't overlook the importance of a comfortable swim cap, which can help reduce drag and keep your hair out of your face, enhancing your focus while swimming.

Training aids can also play a significant role in your development as a swimmer. Tools like pull buoys, kickboards, and fins can help you improve your technique, strengthen specific muscle groups, and build endurance. A pull buoy, for example, can assist in isolating your upper body while allowing your legs to rest, enabling you to focus on your arm strokes and breathing patterns. Kickboards are excellent for developing leg strength and improving your kick technique, while fins can help you swim more efficiently and build speed. Integrating these aids into your training routine can lead to significant improvements in your overall swimming performance.

Lastly, don't forget about the importance of post-swim care. A good towel, ideally one that dries quickly and is compact for easy transportation, will help you transition smoothly from the water to your next discipline. Additionally, consider a waterproof bag to keep your swim gear organized and protected from the elements. Proper care and maintenance of your swim gear will not only prolong its life but also ensure that you are always prepared for your next training session or race. By equipping yourself with the essential swim gear, you will be setting a solid foundation for your journey toward becoming an Ironman athlete.

Must-Have Cycling Equipment

When preparing for your first Ironman, having the right cycling equipment is crucial for achieving both comfort and performance on race day. Unlike traditional road races, an Ironman triathlon demands a unique set of gear that can withstand long hours of training and competition. This subchapter will guide you through the must-have cycling equipment that every first-time Ironman athlete should consider to enhance their experience.

First and foremost, a quality road bike is essential. While you don't need the most expensive model on the market, investing in a bike that fits you well and meets the demands of triathlon racing is important. A triathlon-specific bike is designed for aerodynamics, allowing you to maintain a more efficient position while minimizing wind resistance. If you're unsure about which bike to choose, consider visiting a local bike shop for a professional fitting. This will not only help you select the right frame size but also ensure that your bike is adjusted for optimal comfort and performance during long rides.

In addition to the bike itself, certain accessories can dramatically improve your cycling experience. A good pair of cycling shoes that clip into your pedals will provide better power transfer during your ride. These shoes are designed to work with specific pedal systems, enhancing efficiency and allowing you to pedal with greater force. Furthermore, investing in a comfortable, padded bike seat can make long training sessions more bearable, reducing the risk of discomfort that could hinder your performance. Remember, comfort is key when you're logging hours in the saddle.

Another critical aspect of your cycling setup is hydration and nutrition. As you train for your Ironman, you'll need to stay hydrated and fueled during long rides. A quality hydration system, such as a hydration pack or bike-mounted bottles, will allow you to easily access fluids without breaking your cycling rhythm. Additionally, planning your nutrition strategy is essential; consider packing energy gels, bars, or other easily digestible snacks to maintain your energy levels throughout your ride. Developing a routine for nutrition during training will help you understand what works best for you and ensure you have the right fuel on race day.

Lastly, don't overlook the importance of safety gear. A well-fitting helmet is not just a legal requirement; it's a crucial piece of equipment that protects you in case of accidents. Ensure that your helmet meets safety standards and fits snugly without being uncomfortable. Visibility is also important, so consider wearing bright clothing and using lights or reflectors, especially if you'll be training early in the morning or late in the evening. By prioritizing safety, you can focus more on your training and less on potential hazards.

By equipping yourself with the right cycling gear, you'll set yourself up for success as you embark on your Ironman journey. From selecting a suitable bike to investing in accessories that enhance comfort and performance, every piece of equipment plays a role in your overall experience. Remember that the right gear can make a significant difference in your training and race day performance, so take the time to choose wisely.

Running Gear for Comfort and Performance

When preparing for your first Ironman, the right running gear can significantly enhance both your comfort and performance. As you transition from training to race day, understanding how specific equipment impacts your run can make a notable difference in your overall experience. The importance of investing in quality running shoes cannot be overstated; they are the foundation of your running performance. Look for shoes that offer a good fit, adequate cushioning, and support tailored to your running style. Visiting a specialty running store for a gait analysis can help you choose the perfect pair to prevent injuries and optimize your efficiency during long runs.

In addition to shoes, moisture-wicking apparel plays a crucial role in ensuring comfort during training and racing. Fabrics designed to pull sweat away from the skin can help regulate your body temperature and reduce the risk of chafing, a common issue during long-distance events. Opt for fitted clothing that minimizes excess fabric, which can cause drag and distraction. While many athletes focus on shorts and shirts, don't overlook the importance of quality socks. Invest in socks specifically designed for running to provide cushioning and prevent blisters, which can be a painful setback during your Ironman journey.

Hydration and nutrition gear is another vital aspect of your running setup. As you prepare for the demands of an Ironman, consider using a hydration belt or handheld water bottles to ensure easy access to fluids during your runs. This is especially important for long training sessions, where maintaining hydration levels can make or break your performance. Additionally, explore options for portable nutrition, such as energy gels or chews, to fuel your body during your runs. Practicing your nutrition strategy during training will help you determine what works best for you, so you can execute your plan seamlessly on race day.

As you get closer to the event, consider gear that enhances your visibility and safety, especially if you plan to train during early mornings or evenings. Reflective clothing, headlamps, or clip-on lights can help ensure you are seen by others, reducing the risk of accidents. Furthermore, don't underestimate the benefits of a good running watch. A GPS watch can help you track your distance, pace, and heart rate, allowing you to monitor your training progress effectively. This data can be invaluable for adjusting your training plan and ensuring you're on target for race day.

Finally, remember that comfort is not only about the gear you wear but also how you prepare your body for the Ironman experience. Incorporating gear such as foam rollers and massage balls can aid in recovery and prevent injuries. Prioritize recovery by integrating stretching and mobility work into your routine, which can be further supported by comfortable recovery apparel. By carefully selecting your running gear and considering how it impacts your performance and comfort, you'll be better equipped to tackle the challenges of your first Ironman. Focus on finding the right combination of equipment that supports your individual needs, as this will contribute to a more enjoyable and successful race experience.

Additional Accessories and Gadgets

In the journey to becoming an Ironman athlete, having the right gear is crucial, not only for performance but also for comfort and safety. While the primary equipment—such as a reliable bike, wetsuit, and running shoes—forms the foundation of your training, additional accessories and gadgets can enhance your experience and help you train more effectively. This subchapter delves into essential accessories that every first-time Ironman athlete should consider, ensuring a well-rounded preparation for race day.

One of the most important accessories for any triathlete is a quality heart rate monitor. This device allows you to track your heart rate during training sessions, helping you understand your intensity levels and adjust your workouts accordingly. Staying within your target heart rate zones can significantly improve your endurance and overall performance. Many modern heart rate monitors also come with GPS functionality, providing additional metrics like pace and distance. This data is invaluable for tailoring your training plan and ensuring you are building your stamina effectively across all three disciplines: swimming, cycling, and running.

Another must-have accessory is a multi-sport watch. These devices not only track your performance in each segment of the triathlon but also provide features like interval training, transition timers, and navigation. Investing in a watch that integrates seamlessly with your training apps can also provide you with insights into your progress over time. The data collected from your workouts can inform your nutrition strategies and mental preparation, allowing you to fine-tune your approach to both training and racing. A reliable watch can significantly reduce the stress of managing your time during training sessions and on race day itself.

Nutrition is a pivotal aspect of Ironman training, and having the right tools can make a substantial difference. A portable hydration system, such as a running belt with bottles or a hydration pack for cycling, ensures that you stay hydrated during long training sessions. Additionally, consider investing in a quality blender or meal prep containers for creating and organizing your nutrition plan. A good blender can help you whip up nutrient-dense smoothies or recovery shakes post-workout, while meal prep containers allow you to plan your meals in advance, ensuring you meet your dietary needs throughout your training cycle.

Lastly, mental preparation is often overlooked but is vital for first-time Ironman athletes. Accessories such as journals or mental training apps can help you track your thoughts, set goals, and reflect on your training journey. Visualization techniques can also be enhanced with tools like guided meditation apps or even simple audio recordings that help you focus on your race-day mindset. By integrating these mental training tools into your routine, you'll not only build resilience but also foster a positive attitude towards the challenges that lie ahead.

In conclusion, the right accessories and gadgets can greatly enhance your Ironman training experience. From monitoring your heart rate and performance to ensuring proper nutrition and mental preparation, each tool plays a role in your success. As you embark on this journey, consider how these additional items can support your training and help you overcome common challenges, ultimately preparing you for a triumphant race day.

Chapter 6: Overcoming Common Challenges in Ironman Training

Dealing with Injuries

Dealing with injuries is an inevitable part of the journey for first-time Ironman athletes. Understanding how to manage injuries effectively can make a significant difference in your training and overall performance. The physical demands of an Ironman race place considerable stress on the body, leading to potential injuries ranging from minor aches to more severe conditions. Recognizing the signs of injury early and implementing appropriate strategies can help you stay on track with your training plan and minimize downtime.

First, it's essential to familiarize yourself with common injuries associated with triathlon training. These include overuse injuries such as runner's knee, IT band syndrome, and Achilles tendinitis, as well as acute injuries like sprains or strains. Being aware of the symptoms of these injuries can help you distinguish between normal training discomfort and something that requires immediate attention. If you experience persistent pain that worsens with activity or does not improve with rest, it may be time to consult a healthcare professional for an assessment.

Prevention is the best strategy when it comes to injuries. Incorporating a well-rounded training plan that includes strength training, flexibility exercises, and proper warm-up and cool-down routines can significantly reduce the risk of injury. Additionally, listen to your body and allow for adequate recovery time between workouts. Overtraining is a common pitfall for first-time athletes, so make adjustments to your training schedule as needed, and don't hesitate to take a step back if you notice signs of fatigue or discomfort.

If you do find yourself facing an injury, it is crucial to adopt a proactive approach to recovery. Apply the R.I.C.E. method—Rest, Ice, Compression, and Elevation—to manage minor injuries effectively. This method can alleviate pain and reduce swelling, allowing you to return to training sooner. Also, consider integrating cross-training activities that are low-impact, such as swimming or cycling, to maintain your fitness level while giving the injured area a chance to heal. Consulting a physical therapist can provide tailored rehabilitation exercises and further enhance your recovery process.

Finally, maintaining a positive mental attitude is vital during the injury recovery phase. Injuries can be discouraging and may lead to feelings of frustration or anxiety about your upcoming race. Focus on what you can control and use this time to strengthen other areas of your training, such as nutrition strategies or mental preparation techniques. Stay connected with fellow athletes for support and motivation, and remember that setbacks are a natural part of any athletic journey. With the right mindset and a solid recovery plan, you can bounce back stronger and continue your pursuit of Ironman success.

Time Management for Busy Athletes

For first-time Ironman athletes, mastering the art of time management is crucial to successfully balancing training, work, and personal life. The demands of an Ironman training plan can be overwhelming, especially for those who juggle professional commitments and family responsibilities. Establishing a structured schedule is essential to ensure that training sessions are prioritized while still allowing time for recovery and other obligations. By implementing effective time management strategies, athletes can maximize their training effectiveness and maintain a healthy work-life balance.

Creating a weekly training plan is an excellent starting point for busy athletes. This plan should outline not only the workouts for each day but also allocate time for recovery, nutrition preparation, and any other commitments. Athletes should consider their peak productivity times when scheduling workouts, placing high-intensity sessions during periods of optimal energy levels. Incorporating flexibility into the training schedule can also help accommodate unexpected events that may arise, allowing athletes to adjust their plans without feeling overwhelmed.

Another effective strategy is to utilize time-blocking techniques. This involves assigning specific blocks of time for different activities throughout the day. By doing so, athletes can ensure that they dedicate focused time to their training, work, and personal life, minimizing distractions and enhancing productivity. For instance, early mornings might be dedicated to swim workouts, while evenings could focus on cycling or running. This structured approach can prevent the feeling of chaos that often accompanies training for an Ironman.

Nutrition plays a vital role in an athlete's performance and recovery, and managing time effectively in this area is equally important. Meal prepping can save valuable time during the week, allowing athletes to focus on training without the added stress of daily meal planning. By preparing healthy meals in advance, athletes can ensure they are fueling their bodies appropriately while avoiding the temptation of less nutritious options. Additionally, understanding the importance of hydration and nutrition timing can enhance training outcomes and overall performance during race day.

Finally, mental preparation is an often-overlooked aspect of time management for busy athletes. Taking time for mindfulness practices, such as meditation or visualization, can significantly enhance focus and motivation. Allocating even a few minutes each day for mental conditioning can help athletes stay mentally sharp and resilient throughout their training journey. By integrating these practices into their schedules, athletes not only manage their time more effectively but also cultivate a positive mindset, which is essential for overcoming the challenges that come with preparing for an Ironman.

Staying Motivated During Training

Staying motivated during training is crucial for first-time Ironman athletes, as the journey can be long and demanding. The commitment required to complete an Ironman involves not just physical preparation but also a strong mental resolve. One effective strategy to maintain motivation is to set realistic and achievable goals throughout your training cycle. Breaking down the larger goal of completing an Ironman into smaller, manageable milestones—such as completing your first long run or mastering a specific swim technique—can provide a sense of accomplishment and keep your spirits high. Celebrate these milestones, as each one is a step closer to your ultimate goal.

Another vital aspect of maintaining motivation is establishing a solid support system. Engaging with fellow athletes, friends, and family can create an encouraging environment that fosters accountability. Joining a local triathlon club or participating in group training sessions can help keep you motivated. The camaraderie found in these groups can serve as a powerful motivational force, reminding you that you are not alone in this journey. Sharing experiences, challenges, and successes with others can help you stay focused and inspired, especially during those tough training days when self-doubt may creep in.

Incorporating variety into your training routine can also combat burnout and keep motivation levels high. Repeatedly performing the same workouts can lead to monotony and decreased enthusiasm. To counteract this, try mixing up your training sessions by incorporating different routes for cycling and running, joining swim clinics to learn new techniques, or participating in brick workouts that combine multiple disciplines. Varying your training environment and activities can reignite your excitement and passion for the sport, making each session feel fresh and invigorating.

Nutrition plays a pivotal role in your training motivation. Proper fueling not only enhances your performance but also impacts your mood and energy levels. Develop a nutrition strategy tailored to your training needs, focusing on whole foods that provide sustained energy. Experimenting with different pre- and post-workout meals can help you find what works best for you, ensuring that you feel good during training. Staying hydrated and properly replenishing your body after workouts will help you recover faster and maintain your enthusiasm for training.

Lastly, mental preparation is essential for sustaining motivation. Developing a positive mindset, practicing visualization techniques, and employing mindfulness can significantly impact your training experience. Set aside time for mental training, where you can visualize yourself successfully completing your Ironman. This mental rehearsal can create a powerful sense of confidence and motivation. Additionally, adopting a mantra or positive affirmation can help you push through challenging moments. By equipping yourself with both the mental and physical tools necessary for success, you'll find it easier to stay motivated throughout your Ironman training journey.

Coping with Weather and Environmental Factors

Coping with weather and environmental factors is a crucial aspect of preparing for your first Ironman. As you embark on this challenging journey, understanding how to adapt your training and race day strategies to various weather conditions can significantly influence your performance and overall experience. From scorching heat to sudden rainfall, each environmental aspect presents unique challenges that require thoughtful planning and preparation. This subchapter will equip you with essential strategies for navigating these factors effectively.

When training for an Ironman, it is vital to familiarize yourself with the climate conditions you are likely to encounter on race day. Research the typical weather patterns for the location of your event, including temperature ranges, humidity levels, and the likelihood of rain or wind. This information will help you tailor your training sessions to simulate race conditions. For instance, if you expect high humidity, incorporate longer runs or bike rides during the hottest parts of the day. This acclimatization process will prepare your body for the stressors you will face in the actual race.

Nutrition strategies also play a significant role in coping with environmental factors. Hot and humid conditions can lead to increased perspiration, resulting in a higher loss of electrolytes. Therefore, it's essential to adjust your nutrition plan accordingly. Experiment with hydration methods and electrolyte supplementation during your training to find what works best for you in different weather scenarios. Conversely, in cooler conditions, you may need to consume more calories to maintain body warmth and energy levels. Understanding how your body reacts to various environmental influences will help you optimize your nutrition strategy for race day.

Mental preparation is equally important when dealing with unpredictable weather. The ability to adapt your mindset in response to changing conditions can make all the difference. Practice visualization techniques, imagining yourself successfully navigating adverse weather scenarios. Develop a positive self-talk routine that reinforces your resilience and determination, reminding yourself that you have trained for these challenges. By mentally rehearsing your responses to potential weather-related obstacles, you'll be better equipped to maintain focus and composure during the race.

Lastly, gear essentials must be carefully selected with the weather in mind. Invest in high-quality, weather-appropriate clothing and equipment. For hot conditions, consider moisture-wicking fabrics, breathable shoes, and a reliable hydration system. In cold environments, layering becomes crucial; ensure you have thermal gear that allows for easy removal as you warm up during the race. Additionally, familiarize yourself with how different gear performs in various weather conditions during your training. This knowledge will be invaluable on race day, allowing you to make informed decisions about what to wear and carry, ultimately enhancing your performance and comfort.

Chapter 7: Ironman Race Day Logistics and Tips

Pre-Race Preparation

Pre-Race Preparation is a crucial phase in your journey as a first-time Ironman athlete. The weeks leading up to race day are not just about physical training; they encompass a holistic approach that combines mental readiness, nutrition strategies, gear organization, and logistical planning. Each of these elements plays a significant role in ensuring you arrive at the starting line confident and prepared to tackle the challenges ahead.

First and foremost, mental preparation is paramount. As race day approaches, it's essential to visualize success and cultivate a positive mindset. Engage in mental rehearsals where you envision yourself navigating each segment of the race, from the swim to the bike and finally the run. This technique helps to reduce anxiety and builds confidence. Consider practicing mindfulness or meditation to enhance your focus and resilience, allowing you to tackle any hurdles with a calm and determined attitude.

Nutrition strategies should also be a primary focus during your pre-race preparation. In the weeks leading up to the event, refine your race-day nutrition plan based on your training experiences. Experiment with different foods and hydration methods during long training sessions to find what works best for you. Make a detailed nutrition schedule for race day, ensuring you incorporate a balance of carbohydrates, proteins, and electrolytes. This preparation is essential for maintaining your energy levels and optimizing performance throughout the grueling 140.6 miles.

Equipping yourself with the right gear is another essential component of pre-race preparation. Invest time in selecting and testing your race-day attire, including a comfortable wetsuit, cycling gear, and running shoes that have been broken in during training. Additionally, familiarize yourself with all the equipment you'll be using, from your bike to your hydration system. Ensure that everything is in excellent working order and practice transitions to minimize downtime on race day. This attention to detail can significantly impact your overall performance.

Finally, organizing race day logistics is crucial to reduce stress and ensure a smooth experience. Review the race schedule, including packet pickup, transition setup, and pre-race briefings. Plan your travel to the venue, allowing extra time for unforeseen delays, and consider your accommodation arrangements to ensure you are well-rested. Develop a race day timeline that includes wake-up times, meals, and pre-race warm-ups. Being well-prepared will allow you to focus on your race strategy rather than logistical concerns, ultimately contributing to a more enjoyable and successful Ironman experience.

Race Day Timeline

Race Day is the culmination of months, if not years, of hard work, dedication, and training. For first-time Ironman athletes, having a well-structured timeline on race day can significantly reduce anxiety and enhance performance. This timeline not only helps in organizing your day but also ensures that you stick to your nutrition and gear strategies, both critical for a successful race. Here's a comprehensive breakdown of your race day timeline to help you stay focused and prepared.

Start your race day early. Aim to wake up at least three hours before your wave starts. This allows you enough time to hydrate, enjoy a light breakfast, and mentally prepare. Opt for familiar foods that you've practiced with during your training, such as oatmeal, bananas, or energy bars. It's crucial to avoid trying anything new on race day, as this could lead to gastrointestinal issues. Take this time to visualize your race, reminding yourself of the goals you've set and the training you've completed.

After fueling your body, head to the event site at least two hours before the start. This gives you ample time to set up your transition area. Lay out your gear in a logical order: swim gear, bike equipment, and running shoes. Make sure to check your bike for any last-minute adjustments. Ensure that your nutrition—such as gels, bars, or electrolyte drinks—is easily accessible. Familiarize yourself with the transition layout and practice your transition plan in your mind. A smooth transition can save you precious minutes on race day.

As race time approaches, focus on your mental game. Spend some time warming up, which can include light stretching or a short swim if possible. This not only helps to loosen your muscles but also gets you mentally in the zone. Keep your energy levels up with small snacks, and remember to hydrate. When you hear the announcer call your wave to the start line, take a moment to breathe deeply and center yourself. A positive mindset will set the tone for your race.

During the swim start, maintain a steady pace and stick to your pre-planned strategy. After completing the swim, remember to transition smoothly to the bike. Take a moment to refocus and hydrate before starting the cycling leg. While biking, monitor your effort and nutrition, aiming to consume small amounts of food and drink consistently. As you near the end of the bike portion, prepare for your transition to running, ensuring you have everything you need for the final leg of the race.

Finally, the run is where you can truly embrace the culmination of your efforts. Stay aware of your pacing and listen to your body. Use the nutrition strategies you've practiced and remember to encourage yourself with positive affirmations. As you approach the finish line, soak in the atmosphere; this is the moment you've trained for, and crossing that finish line will be an unforgettable experience. By following this race day timeline, you can optimize your performance and enjoy every moment of your first Ironman journey.

Transition Areas: What to Expect

Transition areas, often referred to as T1 and T2, are critical components of the Ironman race experience. For first-time athletes, these zones serve as the bridge between the three disciplines: swimming, cycling, and running. Understanding what to expect in transition areas can significantly impact your overall race performance and efficiency. Preparation in this aspect is just as crucial as your training for swimming, biking, or running.

Upon entering the transition area after the swim, you will need to quickly shift your mindset from the water to the bike. This can be a disorienting experience, especially after the exertion of the swim. It's essential to familiarize yourself with the layout of the transition area before race day. Look for your designated spot, often marked with a race number.

Knowing the location of your gear will save you valuable time and prevent unnecessary stress when you're transitioning out of the water. As you approach your bike, remember to focus on your breathing and maintain a steady pace to avoid any panic or confusion.

In T1, your primary goal is to prepare for the cycling segment. This involves shedding your wetsuit, putting on your helmet, sunglasses, and biking shoes, and grabbing your nutrition supplies. Consider practicing your transition routine during training sessions to build muscle memory. This can help you execute a faster and more efficient transition on race day. Additionally, have a checklist of your gear to ensure nothing is forgotten in the heat of the moment. Organizing your transition area in a logical manner can also minimize the time spent fumbling for items.

T2, the transition from cycling to running, follows a similar process but with its unique challenges. After dismounting your bike, the shift from cycling to running can feel abrupt. It's important to take a moment to steady yourself before you head to your designated area. Here, you'll need to switch out your biking shoes for running shoes, grab any additional nutrition, and possibly change into a hat or sunglasses if conditions warrant it. Again, practicing this transition during your training can help you recognize how your body feels and what adjustments you may need to make on race day.

The key to mastering transition areas lies in preparation and practice. Visualizing your transitions, knowing the layout, and rehearsing your routine will allow you to remain calm and focused during the race. These moments, although brief, can significantly impact your overall time and mindset as you move through each segment of the Ironman. Embrace the transitions as part of the journey; they are not just logistical hurdles but also opportunities to reset your mind and body before tackling the next challenge.

Post-Race Recovery Strategies

Completing an Ironman is an extraordinary achievement that demands not only rigorous training but also effective post-race recovery strategies. The immediate aftermath of the race is critical for your body to begin the healing process and regain strength. Recovery should start as soon as you cross the finish line. Begin with hydration: rehydrate with water or an electrolyte drink to replenish fluids lost during the race. This initial step is vital to kickstart your recovery and prevent dehydration, which can lead to fatigue and cramping in the days following the event.

After rehydration, focus on nutrition. Your body has just endured a grueling 140.6-mile challenge, and it is essential to provide it with the nutrients it desperately needs. Aim for a balanced meal rich in carbohydrates and protein within 30 minutes of finishing the race. Carbohydrates will help replenish glycogen stores, while protein aids in muscle repair. Snacks such as a banana with nut butter or a protein shake can be convenient options in the hustle and bustle of post-race celebrations. Prioritizing nutrition in the hours following the race will enhance recovery and prepare your body for any upcoming training sessions.

Rest is another critical component of your recovery strategy. Allow your body the time it needs to heal and recuperate. The day after the race, consider engaging in light activities such as walking or gentle stretching to promote blood flow without putting undue stress on your muscles. Avoid high-intensity workouts for at least a week, as your body requires time to recover from the physical toll of the race. Listening to your body during this period is crucial; if you feel soreness or fatigue, grant yourself the grace to rest longer.

Mental recovery is equally important and often overlooked. An Ironman is not just a physical challenge but a psychological one as well. Take time to reflect on your experience—celebrate your accomplishments and acknowledge the challenges you faced. Engage in conversations with fellow competitors or friends about the race, which can help solidify your memories and reinforce your sense of achievement. This mental processing can ease the transition back into regular training and help you set future goals, ensuring that you maintain a positive mindset.

Lastly, as you move beyond immediate recovery, consider setting up a follow-up maintenance plan. This includes incorporating active recovery days into your routine, focusing on flexibility and mobility exercises, and gradually returning to your regular training schedule. Monitor how your body responds during this transition, and be open to modifying your training plan based on your recovery needs. Emphasizing both physical and mental recovery strategies will not only enhance your overall well-being but also prepare you for future endurance challenges.

Chapter 8: Triathlon Swimming Techniques for Beginners

Basics of Freestyle Swimming

Freestyle swimming, often regarded as the most efficient stroke, serves as the cornerstone of your triathlon performance. For first-time Ironman athletes, mastering the basics of this stroke is crucial, as it plays a significant role in your overall race strategy. Freestyle swimming emphasizes streamlined movement, proper body positioning, and effective breathing techniques, all essential for conserving energy and maximizing speed during the swim leg of an Ironman.

To begin with, body position is fundamental in freestyle swimming. A flat and horizontal alignment in the water reduces drag, allowing you to glide more effortlessly. Athletes should strive to maintain a neutral head position, with the eyes looking slightly forward. This posture not only helps with buoyancy but also ensures that the hips remain elevated, promoting an efficient stroke. Engaging your core throughout the swim will further enhance stability, allowing for a more powerful kick and stroke.

Breathing is another critical component of freestyle swimming. Beginners often struggle with this aspect, leading to inefficiencies and fatigue. The key is to develop a rhythmic breathing pattern that enables you to inhale quickly while maintaining your stroke cadence. Athletes should practice bilateral breathing, which involves breathing on both sides. This technique not only promotes symmetry in your stroke but also helps you adapt to varying water conditions, such as waves and currents, during race day.

Furthermore, mastering the arm pull is vital for generating propulsion in the water. The stroke begins with a high elbow entry, leading into a catch phase where the hand extends forward. Athletes should focus on engaging the lats and pulling through the water with a strong, controlled motion. It's essential to avoid overreaching and instead concentrate on an efficient, compact stroke that allows for better energy conservation. Consistent practice, drills, and video analysis can significantly improve your technique and overall performance.

Finally, incorporating proper training plans that focus on freestyle swimming will enhance your readiness for the Ironman swim leg. Regular swim workouts should include drills that emphasize technique, endurance, and speed. Consider joining a local swim group or hiring a coach to refine your skills. Remember, as you progress in your training, nutrition strategies will also play a pivotal role in your swimming performance, ensuring that you are well-fueled and hydrated to tackle the swim with confidence. Embrace the basics of freestyle swimming, and you'll set a strong foundation for a successful Ironman journey.

Improving Technique and Efficiency

Improving technique and efficiency is crucial for first-time Ironman athletes as they prepare for the rigorous demands of race day. Mastering your technique across swimming, cycling, and running not only enhances performance but also conserves energy, allowing you to finish strong. As you embark on your training journey, focus on developing skills that will optimize your movements and reduce fatigue, ensuring that you can tackle the challenges of a full Ironman.

In swimming, technique is paramount. Many novices struggle with buoyancy and stroke efficiency, which can lead to early fatigue. To improve your swimming technique, consider working with a coach or taking lessons that focus on stroke mechanics, breathing patterns, and body positioning. Drills such as catch-up swimming and fingertip dragging can help refine your stroke while increasing your overall efficiency in the water. Additionally, regular practice in open water can familiarize you with race conditions, helping you learn to navigate waves and other swimmers effectively.

Cycling efficiency is equally vital, as you will need to maintain a strong pace over a long distance. Proper bike fit is essential to avoid discomfort or injury and to maximize power transfer from your legs to the pedals. Spend time practicing gear changes and learn to maintain a steady cadence, as this will help you manage your energy throughout the ride. Incorporating interval training can also improve your speed and endurance. Focus on technique by practicing smooth, controlled pedal strokes and using your core to stabilize your body while cycling.

Running, the final leg of the Ironman, demands a balance of endurance and technique. Many first-time athletes experience fatigue during this segment due to inefficient running form. To enhance your running technique, work on your posture, stride, and foot strike. Drills such as high knees, butt kicks, and strides can build strength and develop a more efficient running style. Additionally, incorporating strength training into your routine can improve your overall stability and reduce the risk of injury, allowing you to maintain a strong pace throughout the marathon.

As you refine your technique across all three disciplines, remember that efficiency is not just about physical performance; it's also about mental preparation. Visualization techniques can help you mentally rehearse your movements and anticipate the challenges you might face during the race. Establishing a strong mindset coupled with refined physical skills will empower you to overcome obstacles and maintain focus on race day. By committing to improving your technique and efficiency, you set yourself up for a successful and fulfilling Ironman experience.

Open Water Swimming Tips

Open water swimming can be one of the most daunting aspects of preparing for your first Ironman. Unlike the controlled environment of a pool, open water presents unique challenges such as variable temperatures, currents, and the absence of lane lines. For first-time athletes, mastering open water swimming is essential not only for your performance but also for building confidence. In this section, we will explore practical tips that can enhance your open water swimming experience and help you navigate this crucial leg of the triathlon with greater ease.

To begin, familiarize yourself with the open water conditions where you will be training and racing. This means visiting the location multiple times to assess factors such as water temperature, depth, and potential hazards like rocks or currents. If possible, swim during the same hours you will race to acclimatize your body to the temperature and time of day. Additionally, consider practicing in varying weather conditions, as wind and waves can significantly affect your swimming. The more comfortable you become in different environments, the less likely you will be thrown off by unexpected conditions come race day.

Practicing sighting is another essential skill for open water swimming. In a pool, you can follow the lane lines, but in open water, you need to regularly lift your head to orient yourself towards your destination. This can disrupt your rhythm, so it's important to integrate sighting into your training. Practice lifting your head every few strokes to check your direction, and aim to do this in a way that's smooth and efficient. Additionally, learning to spot landmarks or buoys will help you stay on course without expending unnecessary energy.

Group swims can also enhance your open water experience. Swimming alongside others can help simulate race conditions, allowing you to practice drafting and navigating tight spaces. However, it can also be intimidating if you're not used to the close proximity of other swimmers. To ease any anxiety, start by swimming with a friend or a small group. As you gain confidence, try larger group swims. Remember, the chaos of a mass start can be overwhelming, so practicing your starts in a group setting will help you feel more prepared for the actual race.

Lastly, make sure to integrate proper nutrition and hydration strategies into your open water training sessions. Many athletes underestimate the importance of fueling during long swims, but it's crucial for maintaining energy levels and preventing fatigue. Practice taking in fluids and energy gels while in the water, so you can develop a routine that works for you. This will not only enhance your endurance but will also familiarize you with the process of eating and drinking while swimming, which is vital for race day performance. By following these tips and incorporating them into your training, you will be better prepared to tackle the open water swim portion of your first Ironman with confidence and competence.

Practicing with Purpose

For first-time Ironman athletes, the journey from novice to competitor can be overwhelming. One of the most effective strategies to ensure success is to practice with purpose. This means that every training session should have a specific goal aimed at enhancing performance, building endurance, or perfecting technique. Whether you're honing your swimming skills, cycling longer distances, or increasing your running pace, each workout should be designed to address particular aspects of your preparation. By establishing a clear intention behind each training session, athletes can maximize their time and effort, leading to more significant improvements.

A well-structured training plan is essential for purposeful practice. It is important to break down your workouts into manageable segments that focus on different components of Ironman training, such as endurance, speed, and recovery. For example, your swim sessions could alternate between technique drills and longer endurance swims, while your cycling sessions could include intervals to improve speed and hill workouts for strength. By incorporating variety and specificity into your training regimen, you ensure that each workout contributes directly to your overarching goal of completing your first Ironman.

Nutrition plays a vital role in practicing with purpose. The body requires fuel to perform at its best, and understanding the nutritional needs specific to Ironman training can make a significant difference. Athletes should practice their nutritional strategies during training sessions, experimenting with different foods and hydration methods to see what works best for them. This trial-and-error approach helps identify the optimal fueling strategy for race day, minimizing the chances of gastrointestinal distress or energy depletion during the event. It's not just about what you eat but when you eat; timing your nutrition around your workouts can also greatly enhance performance and recovery.

Mental preparation is just as crucial as physical training. Practicing with purpose should extend to your mental strategies as well. Visualization techniques, positive affirmations, and mindfulness exercises can help build mental resilience and focus. Set specific mental goals for each training session, such as maintaining a positive attitude when the going gets tough or visualizing crossing the finish line. By training your mind alongside your body, you cultivate a mindset that will serve you well on race day, helping you to overcome challenges and maintain motivation throughout the demanding hours of the Ironman.

Finally, remember that purposeful practice also involves learning from each training experience. After every workout, take time to reflect on what went well and what could be improved. Keeping a training journal can help track your progress and identify trends in your performance, allowing you to adjust your training plan as needed. By embracing the concept of practicing with purpose, you not only enhance your physical capabilities but also develop a deeper understanding of yourself as an athlete. This holistic approach will equip you with the tools necessary to tackle the challenges of your first Ironman and emerge victorious.

You Are an Ironman by Creative Pages Publisher

Chapter 9: Cycling Tips for New Ironman Participants

Bike Fit and Comfort

Bike fit and comfort are critical components for first-time Ironman athletes, as they can significantly impact performance and overall enjoyment during training and race day. An improperly fitted bike can lead to discomfort, fatigue, and even injury, making it essential to prioritize proper fit before embarking on extensive training. Understanding the basic elements of bike fit, including seat height, saddle position, and handlebar height, can help you achieve a comfortable and efficient riding position that enhances your endurance and power output.

The first step in achieving a proper bike fit is to adjust the saddle height. A general guideline is to set your saddle so that when your heel is on the pedal at its lowest point, your leg is fully extended. This position allows for optimal leg extension while pedaling, reducing strain on your knees. Additionally, the saddle should be positioned horizontally to ensure that your knees align over the pedals during the stroke. Small tweaks can make a significant difference, so don't hesitate to seek the advice of a professional bike fitter if you're uncertain about your adjustments.

Another crucial aspect of bike fit is saddle comfort. The right saddle can alleviate pressure points and provide support during long rides. Experimenting with different saddle types and widths can help you find one that suits your anatomy. It's also worth considering the angle of the saddle; a slight downward tilt may help relieve pressure on sensitive areas. Remember that comfort on the bike is not just about the saddle; padded shorts, proper chamois, and even the position of your handlebars play a role in your overall comfort level.

Handlebar height and width are also vital for maintaining a comfortable riding posture. If your handlebars are too low, you may be forced into an aggressive position that can lead to neck and back discomfort. On the other hand, handlebars that are too high can result in an inefficient pedal stroke. Aim for a neutral spine position, which allows for better aerodynamics without compromising comfort. Additionally, consider your grip and hand position, as these can affect fatigue levels on longer rides.

Ultimately, achieving the right bike fit involves a combination of personal preference, anatomical considerations, and trial and error. As you prepare for your Ironman, take the time to fine-tune your bike fit to enhance your comfort and performance. Regularly reassess your fit as you build strength and endurance throughout your training journey. A well-fitted bike not only increases efficiency but also fosters a more enjoyable training experience, allowing you to focus on mastering the other facets of your Ironman preparation. However, bike fitting is an art that requires high biomechanical knowledge and getting the fit from a professional at your local bike shop is propably the most recommended as they probably have this knowledge and experience that can save you time and even money even though a bike fit session is not usually cheap.

Building Cycling Endurance

Building cycling endurance is a crucial component of preparing for your first Ironman. As you embark on this journey, understanding the importance of cycling endurance will help you not only complete the race but also do so with efficiency and confidence. Cycling accounts for a significant portion of the Ironman distance, and developing the stamina necessary to sustain your efforts over the long haul is essential. This subchapter focuses on effective training strategies, nutrition tips, and mental preparation techniques to enhance your cycling endurance.

To build cycling endurance, a structured training plan is vital. Begin by incorporating long rides into your weekly schedule, gradually increasing the distance as your fitness improves. Aim for at least one long ride per week, starting at a comfortable distance and adding 10% each week. This incremental approach allows your body to adapt to the demands of longer rides while minimizing the risk of injury. Additionally, consider incorporating back-to-back rides on weekends to simulate race-day fatigue, which will help prepare your body for the challenge ahead.

Nutrition plays a pivotal role in endurance cycling. During your long rides, practice fueling strategies that you plan to use on race day. This includes experimenting with energy gels, bars, and electrolyte drinks to determine what works best for your digestive system. Aim to consume 30-60 grams of carbohydrates per hour of cycling to maintain energy levels and delay fatigue. Don't overlook the importance of hydration; staying properly hydrated will enhance your performance and recovery. Fueling your body correctly during training will not only improve your cycling endurance but also set you up for success on race day.

Mental preparation is often overlooked but is just as important as physical training. Building cycling endurance requires a resilient mindset, especially during those long training sessions when fatigue sets in. Develop mental strategies to push through discomfort, such as setting small goals throughout your ride, using positive self-talk, and visualizing your success. Consider joining a cycling group or finding training partners to create a supportive environment where you can share experiences and motivate each other.

This social aspect of training can alleviate feelings of isolation and enhance your overall endurance training.

Lastly, focus on gear essentials that can support your endurance goals. A properly fitted bike is crucial for comfort and efficiency; investing time and possibly money in a professional fitting can make a significant difference. Additionally, ensure you have the right cycling clothing, such as padded shorts and moisture-wicking fabrics, to enhance your comfort during long rides. Accessories like a reliable bike computer can help you track your distance and speed, allowing for better pacing on long rides. By addressing these elements, you will not only build your cycling endurance but also enjoy the process, making your Ironman training experience more rewarding.

Techniques for Efficient Cycling

For first-time Ironman athletes, mastering cycling techniques is crucial to ensure optimal performance on race day. Cycling efficiency not only affects your overall speed but also preserves energy for the running segment of the race. One essential technique is maintaining a proper cycling position. A well-fitted bike can make a significant difference; ensure your saddle height allows for a slight bend in your knee at the bottom of the pedal stroke, and adjust your handlebar height for comfort and aerodynamics. Keeping a flat back, relaxed shoulders, and a slight bend in the elbows will enhance your efficiency and reduce fatigue.

Pedaling technique is another vital aspect to consider. Aim for a smooth, circular pedal stroke rather than just pushing down on the pedals. Engaging both the upstroke and downstroke will allow you to distribute your energy more evenly, resulting in a more efficient ride. To practice this, incorporate exercises like one-legged pedaling drills into your training routine. These drills will help you focus on the complete circular motion and improve your overall cycling efficiency. Additionally, mastering the art of cadence—typically between 80 to 100 revolutions per minute for endurance cycling—can help maintain a consistent speed without overexerting yourself.

Understanding gear selection and shifting techniques is essential for navigating varied terrain during the Ironman. Familiarize yourself with your bike's gearing system and practice shifting to ensure you can easily change gears as needed. When approaching hills, shift to a lower gear well in advance to maintain momentum without exhausting your legs. Conversely, when descending, shift to a higher gear to take advantage of gravity while keeping your cadence high. This not only conserves energy but also prepares you for the transition from cycling to running, allowing for a smoother shift in muscle engagement.

Incorporating interval training into your cycling routine can significantly enhance your endurance and speed. This involves alternating between high-intensity bursts and recovery periods, which helps build strength and improve your cardiovascular fitness. For example, during a training ride, consider incorporating short sprints followed by a few minutes of easy cycling. Over time, this technique will enable you to handle the physical demands of the Ironman, making you more resilient when faced with long distances and varying terrain on race day.

Lastly, don't underestimate the importance of nutrition and hydration during your cycling training. Developing a strategy for fueling your body before, during, and after rides is crucial for maintaining energy levels and promoting recovery. Experiment with different types of energy gels, bars, or drinks during your training sessions to find what works best for you. Additionally, practice drinking while cycling to ensure you can stay hydrated without compromising your form. By honing these techniques and integrating them into your training plan, you'll be well-prepared to tackle the cycling segment of your first Ironman with confidence and efficiency.

Navigating Different Terrains

Navigating different terrains during Ironman training is crucial for first-time athletes, as each discipline presents unique challenges that can affect performance and overall race day success. Understanding how to effectively tackle varied landscapes—whether they be flat roads, steep hills, or technical trails—will not only enhance your physical abilities but also build confidence as you prepare for the Ironman journey. This chapter will guide you through strategies for swimming in open water, cycling on diverse routes, and running across different surfaces, helping you to become a well-rounded competitor.

In the swimming phase, many first-time athletes find themselves intimidated by the unpredictability of open water. Unlike the controlled environment of a pool, open water can present challenges like waves, currents, and varying temperatures. To navigate these terrains successfully, it's essential to practice sighting techniques, which involve periodically lifting your head to gauge your direction without losing momentum. Incorporating open water swims into your training will help acclimate you to these conditions, allowing you to develop comfort and confidence. Additionally, consider joining local swim groups or participating in practice events to simulate race day conditions and enhance your adaptability.

Cycling is another critical component of the Ironman, and it often takes place on a range of terrains. Whether you are facing flat stretches of road or steep inclines, understanding your bike and how to manage your energy output becomes essential. Training on varied terrains is key to building strength and endurance. For flat routes, focus on maintaining a steady cadence and practicing your nutrition strategy, ensuring you can fuel effectively while riding. For hilly terrains, incorporating hill repeats into your training will prepare your legs for the demands of climbing. Additionally, practicing descents will help you gain confidence and improve your bike handling skills, allowing you to tackle any course with ease.

Running, the final leg of the Ironman, often brings its own set of challenges, particularly when navigating different surfaces such as pavement, trails, or uneven terrain. Each type of surface requires a different approach to stride, pacing, and foot placement. Incorporate a variety of running workouts into your training plan, including long runs on flat roads, tempo runs on trails, and interval training on softer surfaces. This diversity will improve your adaptability and help you develop the muscular endurance needed to conquer the marathon distance at the end of your race. Remember to pay attention to your footwear, as the right shoes can make a significant difference in comfort and performance across different terrains.

As you prepare to tackle these varied terrains, mental preparation plays a critical role in your overall readiness. Familiarizing yourself with the routes you will face on race day can help alleviate anxiety and set realistic expectations.

Visualize yourself navigating through challenging sections, employing techniques that you've practiced during training. Building mental resilience through positive affirmations and visualization can enhance your confidence and ability to remain calm under pressure. Embrace the challenges that come with varying terrains, viewing them as opportunities to grow and improve as an athlete.

In conclusion, navigating different terrains is an integral part of your preparation for the Ironman. By incorporating diverse training strategies into your regimen for swimming, cycling, and running, you will better equip yourself for the challenges ahead. Embrace the learning experience that comes with tackling varied landscapes, as it will ultimately contribute to your success on race day. As you continue your journey, remember that each terrain offers valuable lessons, shaping you into a well-rounded athlete ready to cross the finish line.

Chapter 10: Running Strategies to Complete Your First Ironman

Building a Strong Running Base

Building a strong running base is essential for first-time Ironman athletes, as it lays the foundation for your overall performance on race day. The running segment of an Ironman can be daunting, particularly after the swim and bike portions, but with a well-structured training plan, you can develop the endurance and strength needed to complete this challenge. A solid running base not only enhances your physical capabilities but also boosts your confidence, allowing you to tackle the marathon leg with a positive mindset.

To begin building your running base, focus on gradually increasing your weekly mileage. It is advisable to start with a manageable distance and progressively add mileage each week, typically no more than 10% to prevent injury. Incorporate a mix of short, easy runs and longer, slower-paced runs to develop endurance. Over time, aim to reach a weekly long run that reflects a significant portion of the marathon distance, as this will help your body adapt to the demands of running for extended periods. Consistency is key; establishing a routine will ensure that you steadily build your base without undue stress.

In addition to increasing distance, pay attention to the frequency of your runs. Aim for at least three to four running sessions each week, allowing for adequate rest and recovery. Consider integrating different types of workouts into your training plan, such as tempo runs and interval training. Tempo runs help improve your lactate threshold, while intervals boost your speed and cardiovascular fitness. Incorporating these variations will not only keep your training interesting but also enhance your overall running performance as you prepare for race day.

Nutrition also plays a crucial role in building a strong running base. Proper fueling before, during, and after your runs will help optimize your energy levels and recovery. Carbohydrates are particularly important for endurance athletes, so ensure that your diet includes a good balance of complex carbs, proteins, and healthy fats. Hydration is equally vital; during long runs, practice your hydration strategy to find what works best for you, as staying properly hydrated can significantly impact your performance and recovery.

Lastly, mental preparation is an often overlooked aspect of building a running base. Developing a positive mindset and mental resilience can be just as important as physical training. Visualize your runs, set small, achievable goals, and practice mindfulness techniques to help you stay focused and calm. As you build your running base, celebrate your progress, no matter how small, and remind yourself that each run brings you one step closer to your Ironman goal. With dedication and the right approach, you will set yourself up for success on race day and beyond.

Pacing Strategies for Endurance

Pacing strategies are crucial for first-time Ironman athletes, as they can significantly impact performance and overall race experience. An Ironman race consists of three disciplines: swimming, cycling, and running, each with its own demands and pacing considerations. Establishing a disciplined approach to pacing not only helps manage energy reserves but also enhances the likelihood of a successful finish. This subchapter will explore effective pacing strategies tailored for each segment of the Ironman, ensuring you can maintain a sustainable effort throughout the race.

In the swimming portion, pacing begins well before you enter the water. It's essential to start at a speed that aligns with your training and comfort level. Many first-time athletes make the mistake of starting too aggressively, driven by adrenaline and the excitement of the event. This can lead to early fatigue, which can haunt you in the later stages of the race. Instead, focus on maintaining a steady and controlled pace, using your training swims to gauge your optimal speed. Aim for a consistent stroke rate and breathing pattern to conserve energy for the transition to cycling.

Transitioning to the cycling segment requires a shift in pacing strategy. During the bike leg, the goal is to find a sustainable pace that allows you to cover the distance efficiently while preserving enough energy for the marathon that follows. It's essential to listen to your body and adjust your effort based on the terrain. Flat sections may allow for faster speeds, while climbs require a more conservative approach. Implementing a cadence strategy—aiming for a specific revolutions per minute (RPM)—can help maintain a steady effort throughout the ride. Additionally, practicing your nutrition strategy during training rides is vital. Consuming the right amount of calories and hydration at regular intervals will support your pacing and performance.

As you transition from cycling to running, your pacing strategy will undergo another transformation. The marathon segment of the Ironman is often perceived as the most challenging, especially after a long day of exertion. It's crucial to embrace a conservative approach during the first few miles of the run. Starting too fast can lead to burnout and a significant drop in performance later on. Instead, focus on maintaining a comfortable pace that allows for a negative split—running the second half faster than the first. Utilize walk breaks if necessary, especially at aid stations, to allow for hydration and nutrition without compromising your overall pace.

Mental preparation also plays a vital role in executing effective pacing strategies. Visualization techniques can help you mentally rehearse your race, including how to handle various pacing scenarios. Anticipating challenges, such as fatigue or adverse weather conditions, and formulating a plan on how to respond can provide reassurance during critical moments. Additionally, surrounding yourself with a supportive community can bolster your confidence and commitment to your pacing strategy. Engaging with fellow athletes or joining training groups can foster accountability and motivate you to adhere to your pacing plan.

In conclusion, effective pacing strategies are integral to the success of first-time Ironman athletes. By understanding the unique demands of each race segment and adopting a disciplined approach to pacing, you can enhance your performance and enjoyment of the event. Incorporating strategies for swimming, cycling, and running, while also emphasizing mental preparation and community support, will equip you with the tools needed to navigate the challenges of Ironman training and racing. Remember, the goal is not just to finish but to finish strong, and pacing will be your ally in achieving that objective.

Techniques for Running Off the Bike

Techniques for running off the bike are crucial for first-time Ironman athletes, as the transition from cycling to running can be one of the most challenging aspects of the race. This phase, often referred to as the "brick" workout, requires specific strategies and techniques to help you prepare both physically and mentally. Understanding how to effectively manage this transition can significantly improve your performance on race day and set you up for success.

One key technique for running off the bike is to incorporate brick workouts into your training regimen. These sessions typically involve cycling followed immediately by running, simulating the race-day experience. Start with shorter distances and gradually increase them as your body adapts to the unique demands of transitioning between disciplines. This not only conditions your muscles but also helps you develop a mental framework for tackling the challenges you will face during the Ironman. Aim to practice these workouts at least once a week, varying the intensity and duration to build endurance and familiarity.

Another important aspect of running off the bike is managing your pace. After hours of cycling, your legs may feel heavy and unresponsive when you first start running. To counteract this, focus on running at a slower pace than your goal race pace for the first few miles. This allows your body to adjust and prevents premature fatigue. Consider using a heart rate monitor to help you gauge your effort level, ensuring that you are not pushing too hard too soon. By starting conservatively, you can gradually increase your speed as you settle into your rhythm.

Nutrition and hydration play pivotal roles in your performance when transitioning from cycling to running. Be sure to practice your nutrition strategy during brick workouts, as what you consume on the bike will directly impact your running ability. Experiment with different types of energy gels, bars, and hydration options to find what works best for you. Additionally, be mindful of your fluid intake; staying adequately hydrated before and during the bike portion will help reduce the likelihood of cramping and fatigue during the run. Fine-tuning your nutrition strategy in training will help you feel more confident and prepared on race day.

Finally, mental preparation is essential when it comes to running off the bike. The physical demands of the Ironman can be overwhelming, and maintaining a positive mindset is crucial. Visualize yourself successfully transitioning from the bike to the run, and practice positive self-talk during your training. Developing mental resilience through techniques such as mindfulness or meditation can help you stay focused and composed when faced with the challenges of race day. By mentally preparing yourself to embrace the discomfort and fatigue, you can enhance your performance and enjoy the experience of completing your first Ironman.

Mental Strategies for the Marathon

As you prepare for your first Ironman, it's essential to recognize that physical training is only one component of your success. The mental aspect of endurance racing is equally crucial, especially during the marathon segment of the event. Mental strategies can help you navigate the challenges you'll encounter on race day, maintain focus, and push through discomfort. Developing a strong mindset will not only enhance your performance but will also make the experience more enjoyable.

One effective strategy for mental preparation is visualization. Athletes often use this technique to mentally rehearse their performance, envisioning themselves successfully completing the marathon. Take time during your training to picture yourself crossing the finish line, feeling strong and accomplished. Visualizing the race can help condition your mind to respond positively to the demands of the event. Consider incorporating this practice into your routine by setting aside a few quiet moments each week to focus on your goals and imagine the sensations of running the marathon.

Another vital mental strategy is the use of positive self-talk. The marathon will undoubtedly present moments of doubt and fatigue, but how you respond in those moments can make a significant difference. Cultivate a repertoire of affirmations that resonate with your goals and training experiences. Phrases like "I am strong" or "I can do this" can serve as powerful reminders of your capabilities. During challenging segments of the race, repeat these affirmations to yourself, allowing them to bolster your confidence and keep your spirits high.

Establishing a race-day mantra can also be beneficial. A mantra is a short, powerful phrase that you can repeat to yourself during the race to maintain focus and motivation. Choose a few words that encapsulate your determination and commitment to completing the marathon. This simple tool can be incredibly effective when the fatigue sets in or when mental fatigue tries to overtake your focus. Having a mantra ready will provide you with a mental anchor to draw upon during tough moments.

Lastly, practice mindfulness techniques throughout your training. Mindfulness, the practice of being present and fully engaged in the moment, can help you manage anxiety and maintain your focus during the marathon. Techniques such as deep breathing, body scans, or simply checking in with your thoughts and feelings can ground you when the race becomes overwhelming. By developing these mental habits before race day, you'll be better equipped to handle the marathon with a clear mind and a confident attitude.

Embracing these mental strategies will not only enhance your performance but will also contribute to a more fulfilling Ironman journey.

Chapter 11: Conclusion and Final Thoughts

Reflecting on Your Journey

Reflecting on your journey as you prepare for your first Ironman is not just about looking back at the miles you've logged or the early mornings you've embraced; it's an opportunity to acknowledge the growth and transformation you've undergone throughout your training. As a first-time athlete, it's essential to take a moment to appreciate the commitment you've made to a challenging but rewarding goal. This reflection can help solidify the lessons learned and foster a positive mindset that will carry you through race day and beyond.

Your training plan has likely been filled with peaks and valleys, from the exhilaration of completing a long run or swim to the struggles of overcoming fatigue or injury. Each of these experiences contributes to your overall resilience and mental fortitude. By revisiting your training log, you can identify patterns in your performance, recognize the improvements you've made, and understand the challenges you've faced. This self-assessment not only highlights your physical progress but also reinforces the mental strategies you've developed to cope with adversity, preparing you for the unpredictable nature of race day.

Nutrition strategies play a critical role in your training and recovery process. Reflecting on what has worked for you—be it specific fueling techniques during long workouts or post-exercise recovery meals—can provide valuable insights. Consider how your dietary choices have affected your performance and overall energy levels. Perhaps you've discovered the importance of hydration or learned to fine-tune your carbohydrate intake. Documenting these insights will enable you to create a personalized nutrition plan that optimizes your performance during the Ironman, ensuring that you are well-fueled and ready to tackle the race.

Gear essentials are another key aspect of your journey that deserves reflection. The equipment you chose to invest in—from your bike to your wetsuit—has likely influenced your confidence and comfort in training. Take the time to evaluate how each piece of gear has performed for you. Were there any adjustments you needed to make for comfort? Did certain items enhance your training experience? By assessing your gear choices, you can ensure that you are well-prepared for race day, equipped with the tools that best support your performance.

Finally, reflecting on the common challenges you faced during your training can empower you to approach race day with a proactive mindset. Whether it was dealing with self-doubt, managing injuries, or balancing your training with personal and professional commitments, acknowledging these hurdles can help you devise strategies to overcome them on race day. By recognizing how you have navigated these challenges, you can enter the race with confidence, armed with the knowledge that you have already triumphed over adversity in your journey to becoming an Ironman athlete. Embrace your journey, celebrate your progress, and use these reflections to propel you toward success.

The Ironman Community

The Ironman community is a vibrant and supportive network that plays a crucial role in the journey of first-time athletes. This community comprises individuals from diverse backgrounds, all united by a shared passion for endurance sports. Whether you are a seasoned triathlete or someone just beginning their Ironman training, being part of this community can enhance your experience, providing motivation, camaraderie, and invaluable resources. The connections formed within this community can make the demanding process of preparing for an Ironman more manageable and enjoyable.

Engaging with fellow athletes can lead to a wealth of shared knowledge. Many first-time participants benefit from the experiences of those who have completed the event before. From training plans tailored for various skill levels to nutrition strategies that have proven successful, the community acts as a treasure trove of information. Local clubs often host training sessions, workshops, and seminars that cover essential topics such as swimming techniques, cycling tips, and running strategies, allowing newcomers to learn from seasoned veterans. This collaborative spirit fosters an environment where athletes can ask questions, share tips, and encourage one another.

Mental preparation and mindset are equally critical elements of Ironman training, and the community plays a significant role in this aspect as well. Many athletes experience self-doubt and anxiety as race day approaches. Within the Ironman community, you'll find plenty of individuals who understand these feelings and can offer advice on overcoming mental barriers. Sharing personal stories of triumph and failure helps to normalize the challenges faced in training and competition. The encouragement and camaraderie found in group settings can significantly bolster your confidence, reminding you that you are not alone in your journey.

In addition to emotional support, the community is also a great resource for practical advice regarding gear essentials. First-time Ironman athletes often feel overwhelmed by the myriad of equipment options available. Fellow athletes can provide insights into what gear is truly necessary, helping to streamline the purchasing process. From wetsuits to bikes, the recommendations from experienced triathletes can guide you toward making informed choices that fit your needs and budget. Moreover, local clubs often organize group buys or second-hand sales, making it easier to acquire essential gear without breaking the bank.

Lastly, the Ironman community thrives on sharing race day logistics and tips that are vital for a successful event. Understanding what to expect on race day can alleviate much of the stress associated with the competition. Participants can share their experiences with transition areas, hydration strategies, and pacing techniques. Many clubs also organize mock races, allowing first-timers to familiarize themselves with the race environment. This preparation fosters not only a sense of belonging but also equips athletes with the knowledge to tackle the challenges of an Ironman race day confidently. Embracing the support of the Ironman community can transform your experience, making it more enjoyable and ultimately leading to a successful first finish.

Embracing Future Challenges

As you embark on the journey to complete your first Ironman, it is crucial to recognize that the path ahead is filled with challenges that will test your physical, mental, and emotional limits. Understanding and embracing these challenges is a central part of your preparation. The training will be demanding, and obstacles may arise, but each challenge presents an opportunity for growth and resilience. Preparing for these hurdles will not only enhance your performance but also deepen your commitment to the Ironman experience.

One of the most significant challenges you may face is the sheer volume of training required. Balancing your training schedule with work, family, and other commitments can feel overwhelming. It is essential to develop a structured training plan that allows flexibility while ensuring you stay on track. This plan should include not only the physical workouts but also rest days and recovery strategies. Remember, consistency is key, and adapting your plan to fit your lifestyle will help you maintain motivation and prevent burnout.

Nutrition is another critical area where challenges can arise. As you ramp up your training intensity and duration, your nutritional needs will change significantly. It's vital to educate yourself on optimal fueling strategies to sustain your energy levels and promote recovery. Experiment with different foods and hydration strategies during training to determine what works best for your body. This proactive approach will help you avoid gastrointestinal issues on race day, ensuring you can perform at your best when it matters most.

Mental preparation is often overlooked but is equally vital to your success. Training for an Ironman is as much a mental challenge as it is a physical one. You may encounter moments of self-doubt, fatigue, and frustration. Developing a strong mindset through visualization techniques, positive affirmations, and mindfulness practices can help you navigate these mental hurdles. Embrace the power of mental resilience, and remember that each setback is a stepping stone to greater strength and confidence as you approach race day.

Finally, the logistics of race day itself can present a unique set of challenges. From organizing your gear to understanding the course layout, having a comprehensive plan in place is essential. Familiarize yourself with the race environment in advance, including transition areas and hydration stations. Preparing for potential weather changes and knowing how to adapt your gear and strategies accordingly will also be beneficial. Embracing these logistical challenges with confidence and a clear plan will maximize your performance and enhance your overall experience as a first-time Ironman athlete.

Training Plans for Beginners

In this last section of the book, you can find different training plans for first-time Ironman athletes that are free and adaptable to each person. As mentioned earlier in this book, having a coach that guides you through the whole preparation process is super important, however many people either cannot afford it or have promised themselves they will do everything on their own. In that case, feel free to use these plans and/or email creativepagespublisher@gmail.com or send a direct message on Instagram (@creativepagespublisher) for any question you might have.

1. **BeginnerTriathlete.com**
    - **Plan Name:** *20-Week Ironman Training Plan*
    - **Duration:** 20 weeks
    - **Overview:** A structured plan that includes detailed workouts focusing on swim, bike, and run. It's designed for first-timers and progresses gradually.
    - **Pros:** Great for those looking for a simple yet comprehensive guide. Includes heart rate zone training for optimal performance.
    - **Where to Find** (scan the QR code below): BeginnerTriathlete.com

2. **MyProCoach by Phil Mosley**
    - **Plan Name:** *Beginner 16-Week Ironman Plan*
    - **Duration:** 16 weeks
    - **Overview:** Created by professional triathlon coach Phil Mosley, this plan is designed to help you complete your first Ironman with a balance between endurance training and recovery. The plan includes a combination

of swim, bike, run workouts, and strength training sessions.

- **Pros**: Focuses on time-efficient training for those with busy schedules, making it ideal for athletes with limited time.
- **Where to Find (scan the QR code below)**: MyProCoach

3. 220 Triathlon

- **Plan Name**: *Beginner Ironman Training Plan*
- **Duration**: 36 weeks
- **Overview**: This is a comprehensive 36-week plan aimed at first-time Ironman athletes. It includes a progressive build-up of swim, bike, and run training, along with strength sessions. The plan is broken into three phases: base, build, and peak, ensuring gradual progression to avoid injury.

- **Pros**: Provides detailed week-by-week guidance, flexible enough for different fitness levels, and includes tips on pacing and nutrition.
- **Where to Find**: 220 Triathlon - Free Ironman Training Plan

4. BeginnerTriathlete.com

- **Plan Name**: *Free 20-Week Beginner Ironman Training Plan*
- **Duration**: 20 weeks
- **Overview**: This plan is specifically tailored for first-time Ironman athletes, with a focus on gradually increasing volume and intensity. It covers swim, bike, run, and includes flexibility for scheduling around a busy lifestyle. It also offers detailed workouts, including intervals, long-distance endurance sessions, and rest days
- **Pros**: Great for beginners with a structured, easy-to-follow plan. Includes access to the BeginnerTriathlete community for support and advice.

You Are an Ironman by Creative Pages Publisher

- **Where to Find:** BeginnerTriathlete - Free Ironman Plan

You Are an Ironman by Creative Pages Publisher

CP
CREATIVE PAGES

THANK YOU!

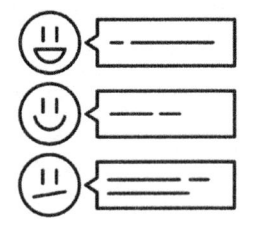

Creative Pages Publisher is thankful for having you as a reader. If you enjoyed this book and/or think there is something to be improved please help us by leaving a review on Amazon. We highly appreciate it!

You Are an Ironman by Creative Pages Publisher

FIND OTHER BOOKS FROM CREATIVE PAGES ON AMAZON.COM WITH THESE QR CODES

You Are an Ironman by Creative Pages Publisher

121

You Are an Ironman by Creative Pages Publisher

You Are an Ironman by Creative Pages Publisher

Thank You for Choosing Creative Pages!

We hope you enjoyed your reading experience with us! Your feedback is incredibly valuable and helps us continue to bring you the best in journals and books. Here's how you can support us:

1. Leave a Review

Your honest review helps other readers find our books and allows us to improve our offerings. If you enjoyed your purchase, please consider leaving a review on Amazon.

2. Follow Us on Instagram

Stay updated on new releases, special offers, and behind-the-scenes content by following us on Instagram: @creativepagespublisher. Join our community and be part of our creative journey!

3. Get in Touch

We'd love to hear from you! For any questions, feedback, or collaborations, feel free to email us at creativepagespublisher@gmail.com.

Thank you for your support and happy reading!

CREATIVE PAGES

You Are an Ironman by Creative Pages Publisher

Disclaimer:

This book has been crafted with the assistance of artificial intelligence alongside the author. While AI has played a significant role in shaping the content, the primary goal of this work is to deliver valuable and original material to the reader. The content presented in this book is intended to be informative and engaging, and every effort has been made to ensure it does not infringe upon or appropriate the intellectual property of others. If you have any concerns regarding the content, please contact the author or publisher directly.

Printed in Great Britain
by Amazon